Journeys with Charley and Beyond

Poetic Memoir - Part Three

JANET CAMERON HOULT

outskirts
press

Journeys with Charley and Beyond
Poetic Memoir - Part Three
All Rights Reserved.
Copyright © 2024 Janet Cameron Hoult
v2.0

This is a work of poeticized non-fiction. The opinions expressed in this manuscript are solely the opinions of the author and do not represent the opinions or thoughts of the publisher. The author has represented and warranted full ownership and/or legal right to publish all the materials in this book.

This book may not be reproduced, transmitted, or stored in whole or in part by any means, including graphic, electronic, or mechanical without the express written consent of the publisher except in the case of brief quotations embodied in critical articles and reviews.

Outskirts Press, Inc.
http://www.outskirtspress.com

ISBN: 978-1-9772-5946-2

Cover Photo © 2024 www.gettyimages.com. All rights reserved - used with permission.

Outskirts Press and the "OP" logo are trademarks belonging to Outskirts Press, Inc.

PRINTED IN THE UNITED STATES OF AMERICA

Dedication

To the Culver City Education Foundation
for its support of
Culver City Unified School District
educational programs
and teaching innovations
which enrich the education
of more than 7,000 students.

Table of Contents

Introduction
Great Performance at the Hollywood Bowl 1
Stages in the Development of a Rocket Scientist 2
Aero Bracero 3

Marriage with Charley
LOVE! 4
Why Does He Love Me? 4
Culver City? Yes! 5
Wrong? Who? Me? 6
My Spicy Food Guy 7
Name Change 8
Wedding Anniversary 9

Rocket Science and Technology
Engineering Rockets 10

Rocket Competitions
Silver Bullet 11

Experimental Sounding Rocket Team (ESRA) – CSULB

Armando Fuentes
Lift Off 12
Landing 12

Haiku by Charles Hoult
Liftoff – 2003 13
The Next Frontier – 2013 13

Space
Mars and The Blood Moon 14
Keyhole Sunset 15

Asteroids

Unwelcome Visitor 16
In Defense of Earth 17

The Natural History Museum

Swirling Ammonites 18
Puffed Up Rock 19
Fool's Gold 20

Family
Son David

Happy Birthday David 22
Bonus Mom 23

Niece Christina

Hang In There! 24

Pamela

I Had a Dream 25
Unwed Motherhood 26
Meeting with Daughter 28
Unwed Grandmotherhood 29
Thanks for Being Lutheran 30

Pamela's Poems

Charley's Family

Little Girls Lost 33
Are You Sleeping God? 34

Grammy to Lots of Kids

Janet's Early Travels

Learning to Drive 36
Flying High 37
Le Twist 38
The Queen and I 39
ROLEX!? 40

Culver City – An Inspiration

    Ode To Janet 41
    2022 Memory Inspiration 42

Sharing with Charley

    What's in a Name – Congress 43

Travels With Charley
Big Bear

    Quaking in Big Bear?? 44
    A Memorable Winter in Big Bear 45

Las Vegas

    Goose Eggs 46

Russia

    A Prayer to St. Catherine, Patron Saint of Maidens 47
    Russian Birches 48

Portugal

    Cork Trees 49

Spain

    Say What???? 50

Solar Eclipses

    Where Did the Sun Go? 51
    Islands 52
    Hawaiian Melodies I'll Remember 53
    Kobe - Limerick 54

Losing Charley

    The Field of Reeds 55
    Touching 56
    Charley Sets Sail 57
    Unexpected Note 58

Acknowledgments 59

Introduction

"Jaunts with Janet" and "Juggling with Janet" – Parts One and Two of my Poetic Memoir – took us on many interesting and exciting adventures. You saw how I managed to "juggle" what life handed me and how I determined that I would survive despite having so many cards stacked against me. When I met Charley a new world opened for me, and our 25 years together were the happiest of my life as we were there for each other in our many activities, provided support during the family crises, and never stopped loving each other. Indeed, the "Great Performance" from Charley when we began our romance and our journeys together is still in my heart.

Great Performance at the Hollywood Bowl

It was our first official date
and the venue was just great
Both lovers of music classical
the Bowl would prove quite magical

The LA Phil had on the bill
music by our favorite musicians
Perhaps it was fate
to know that we
were adhering to our traditions
The music was delightful
romantic and insightful
as the orchestra provided its renditions

We were aware of each other
sitting closely together
in extremely comfortable positions
We smiled as we clapped
then before the second half
he took my hand after intermission
Charley looked into my eyes
then to my surprise
he brought my hand to his lips
and gave it a kiss

The orchestra was superb
but my heartbeat was difficult to curb
after the Great Performance by
my future husband, Charles…!

Stages in the Development of a Rocket Scientist

Read at the AIAA Region VI Student Conference in Tempe, Arizona, April 2008
to Charley Hoult, my terrific husband and rocket science engineer

Elementary School

He shot a spitball in the air, it could have landed anywhere
Upon the floor or on a chair but wound up in his teacher's hair.

Middle School

He and his brother teased their sister, she was lucky that they missed her
When firecrackers on projectiles tossed her dollhouse parts for miles.

High School / College

He learned to fly the little planes that took him in the air
Then yearned to go much higher yet into the stratosphere
In aero engineering he learned how rockets fly
And then he knew his expertise was really flying high.

U.S. Air Force

He launched rockets in those days and tried to ensure that they went the ways
He had carefully programmed them for, so they didn't wind up on the desert floor.

Aerospace / NGST / NASA

He found that launching things is great as long as they go nice and straight
Right where they are supposed to go, then it's really spectacular – a super show!
But if they stray and go awry and get lost up in the sky
Then Houston, Kennedy, and all, "We have a problem," and it's not small.

Retired / University Mentor

Now mentoring student engineers, all of them budding rocketeers
He guides their work and helps them plan to make their rockets safely land

His eyes are dim, his hair is white, but it is with great delight
That he can see what he is teaching to his students will be far-reaching

Into the sky and out into space on rocket ships built with technical grace
To take us to asteroids and to Mars, then carry us far beyond the stars.

Aero Bracero

Charley began his aerospace career while he was studying at MIT. He joined the Air Force and during the Korean War found himself working as an aerospace engineer focused on rockets at Air Force bases throughout the U.S.

All the years I knew Charley
I learned about his career
His focus on aerospace
And his world as an engineer

As a kid, he was into science
And learned all that he could
Then when he went to MIT
He knew that he would
Have rockets as his focus
As he studied Aerospace Engineering
Which he knew he should

Over the years he had positions
With many aerospace firms
Including TRW, Northrop Grumman
and The Aerospace Corporation

Charley also had his own consulting business
Where he could assist groups like JPL
And work on a variety of projects
Like the James Webb Space Telescope

Charley spent time with so many
Different firms in aerospace
He often referred to himself
As an "Aero Bracero" …!

A few poems will introduce you to Charles Pomeroy Hoult. He never cared for his middle name and went by Charles P. Hoult. He also thought that "Charlie" was too "girlie" and preferred to be "Charley," which is what we all called him.

Marriage with Charley

LOVE!

In 1990 when Charley came into my life
I began to realize just what I had missed.
LOVE, not accompanied by strife,
really did exist!

Why Does He Love Me?

With apologies to Elizabeth Barrett Browning

Why does he love me? I shall count the ways
He loves the way I'm there to comfort him
When he's been feeling down and grim
He loves me through the nights and days
I care for him when he feels ill
I think he loves my aging beauty
And when I do my wifely duty
I know he loves me for my skills
He loved me then so long before
We had to face the storms we've weathered
Today I know he loves me more
For after all these years together
It's clear that we both know the score
There is no doubt – we love each other.

Culver City? *Yes!*

When Charley asked me to marry him
I told him I would say "Yes"
If he met just one condition

I watched his face as he waited
And I'm sure his breath was bated
As I gave him this rendition

"Your house in Westwood was your late wife's
I really don't want to live there – too much strife
So here's my condition to saying 'Yes'
Move to Culver City, change your address
We'll be happy here together
Where I've lived for 20 years"

So we both said "Yes" and he moved
To the town that we both loved.

Wrong? Who? Me?

My husband has a policy of never being wrong
It comes up so often it could become a song
For he's a rocket scientist who's sure he's always right
I listen and keep quiet, so we won't have a fight
There are times I must insist that what I say is true
Getting him to agree with me is *hard,* I'm telling you
Some of what he says should probably be censored
Yet his usual response is that he "misremembered."

My Spicy Food Guy

He likes to eat at restaurants
Especially Asian ones
He loves the spicy food they serve
I go along for fun

The spicier the better
Is the food he'll pick
Too many spices on my food
Always makes me sick

Thai, Indian, or Vietnamese
Is where he'll choose to go
And me, I go along with him
Just PHO SHO…!

Name Change

When we met, I was a professor at CSULA. It didn't take long for us to realize that we were going to become a couple, so we began to look at ways to introduce each other to our professional lives. He invited me to rocket events, and I invited him to campus. On his first visit one of the students called him "Mr. Fisher," and the look he gave me was priceless. I corrected the student and also my name ... I became Dr. Janet C. Fisher-Hoult.

Contests were part of the University effort
We always needed judges
So Charley became one of the group
And we really enjoyed having him in the loop

To judge debates and essays by students
To give them ideas beyond the rudiments
Which got him involved with the Engineering Department
And the Rocket Team which he helped start

When emphasis changed to solar cars
He didn't want to be caught in any University "wars"
So began to focus on CSULB
Where he became an adjunct professor
And helped many student rocket engineers
Achieve their goals throughout the years.

Wedding Anniversary

*Thoughts on an invitation
to a 50th wedding anniversary*

My husband has been married
Longer than our friends
It's just that his earlier marriages
All came to different ends
His first one lasted for twelve years
His second lasted three
His third was for fifteen years
And then he married me
We've been married 23 years
The sum is now fifty-three
So he's been married a long, long time
To four women – three plus me …!

Rocket Science and Technology

WWW.RsandT.com is the website for Rocket Science and Technology, which was established and operated by Charles Hoult / Charley. RST continues to provide free analysis tools for the serious amateur rocket designer and university rocket engineering student. Most RST codes consist of an MS Excel file that generates numerical results plus one or more MS Word documents documenting the theoretical basis for the corresponding Excel file. These codes were developed over several years to support various student rocketry projects at two California State University campuses, Los Angeles (CSULA) and Long Beach (CSULB), including competitions managed by the Experimental Sounding Rocket Association (ESRA), the Intercollegiate Rocket Engineering Competition (IREC), and other projects funded by the California Launch Vehicle Education Initiative (CALVEIN) and CSULA.

If you find the software useful, your voluntary contribution to the CSULB Mechanical and Aerospace Engineering (MAE) Department or the CSULA Mechanical Engineering Department would be appreciated in this time of shrunken education budgets. The website includes the following dedication by Charley as well as my Engineering Rockets poem.

This website is dedicated to Dr. Janet Cameron Hoult, my wife, soul mate, and boon companion. She has been a den grandmother to a whole generation of aerospace engineering students who have gained much from her insights, warmth, and wisdom.

Engineering Rockets

Written for the 2009 ESRA banquet
Now that our rockets are back down on Earth
We gather for our banquet with great delight and mirth
And to talk about apogees, nose cones and tail fins
Burn outs, launch rails and problems with winds
The causes of the difficulties with the ignition
And the end of another terrific IREC competition
We knew we had completed well-engineered tasks.
Yet the question was raised – "Who won?" was asked.
The answer is "We all did." By learning from each other
And knowing that we'll spend the year preparing for another
As we learn to build, test, perfect, and eventually fly
More experimental-sounding rockets up in the sky.

Rocket Competitions

Silver Bullet

June 2013 – 8th Annual IREC

Tall, shining, silver bullet
Reaching for the sky
These western plains echo
With the sounds of bullets –
A gunfight at the O.K. Corral –
Now a countdown to a liftoff to the sky

The rocket,
Slender pointer against the mountains, waits ...
Crew members scurry around its base
One adjustment
Then another –
A check on the nose
Lightly powdered by the arid desert dust

54321 blastoff ... 1 second 2 seconds
It's looking good
A blast –
The rocket veers to one side
Pieces fall
The fins –
The skin –
A "perfect" launch
But the rocket died

Who has the answers?
What Lone Ranger can ride in
And solve the riddle
Of what plagues the silver bullet?

Will it be you?

Experimental Sounding Rocket Team (ESRA) – CSULB

During the years I supported and accompanied Charley and his rocket engineering teams, I found I had a special role to play…I became the "grandmother" for the teams. Grandmas always want to make sure their kids remember to have plenty of water, food, and lots of sunscreen when they're launching their rockets in the desert. I also discovered that some of our student rocket engineers were poets as well. Here are two written by a graduate of CSULB.

Armando Fuentes

Lift Off

When it lifts off, our hopes and dreams go with it
As its fuel becomes depleted, its ultimate purpose in life is slowly revealed
For a microsecond it gasps for air, looking for one last kick
Near apogee, it achieves omniscience, it can see all
It culminates its ascension with great pride
From this point on only memories remain
Going down, the end is inevitable
A new journey, a new destiny will begin
Spawned from its remains, a new life has emerged
Ecstatic and curious, like those before it

Landing

Despite zero inherent artistry
it sings away from the pad smoothly
as if enjoying a newly baked pastry
a melodic roar of true beauty
such is its path into history
though its engine is short-lived
it's always a poetic feeling when it is retrieved
whether barely above the ground or in space
and regardless if its parachute is still in place
it dances its way down with grace
striking the ground with elegance
like a violinist striking his chords with masterful pace

Haiku by Charles Hoult

For many years I reminded Charley that we all have poetic souls, even engineers and rocket scientists. After Armando wrote his poems, Charley tried his hand at haiku, and here they are – both "well-engineered!"

Liftoff – 2003

With sudden thunder
Starship, balanced on bright fire,
Seeks the far cosmos

The Next Frontier – 2013

High blue, pierced by a
Silent smoke trail pointing the
Way to distant Mars

Charley and I were both fascinated with space – he as an aerospace engineer and rocket scientist and me as a poet – although I was able to convince him and some of his students that engineers are poets too!

Space

Our fascination with space took us on many trips and we added a few telescopes to our collection. The AstroScan that we took with us on eclipse trips was donated to our local school district Astronomy teacher.

Mars and The Blood Moon

Do you see Mars
over there
peeking at the Moon
as if
he didn't care...
yet watching to see
if she would show herself
to be as bloody
as he?

Mars has lurked for days
in the night sky
looking at the Moon.
Need we wonder why?
The warrior looks for blood...
To win, means some must die.

Mars,
be advised
to keep your distance
or you will meet
with great resistance.
We wish our
Moon's beams
to light
the night
with
silver
streams
that
bring
delight.

Keyhole Sunset

When I taught poetry classes I focused on more than just literary devices – although you could "shape poems" in that category!

The sun,
balancing
on the horizon,
filters through
a dark marine haze
and resembles
a keyhole
waiting
for
some
one
to
open
the
sky

Asteroids

*LA Times 10/17/2021: NASA's Lucy, with diamonds, on an asteroid trek 10/16/2021
NASA planned to launch another mission the following month to
test whether humans might be able to alter an asteroid's orbit –
practice in case Earth ever has a killer rock headed this way.*

Unwelcome Visitor

Inspired by Dr. William Ailor's AIAA talk "An Overview of Planetary Defense"

When an asteroid is on the way
We sure don't want it to spoil our day
We could deflect it with an impulsive push
And give it a shove right on its tush!
We could look at ways to ensure a wide berth
But it may be easier just to move Earth!

In Defense of Earth

Inspired by Dr. Nahum Melamed's AIAA talk on Planetary Defense
"Near Earth Object NEO Disaster Plan"

For effective mitigation
We need early detection
Of the asteroids that could hit our Earth.

So we do our observation
And determine characterization
Of the asteroids that are circling Earth.

We take into consideration
The thermal radiation
The asteroid population could inflict on Earth.

Just think of the destruction
If one landed in the ocean
A tsunami with waves of giant girth!

So we need the position at detection
To determine the best deflection
And then decide how many craft to launch from Earth.

But it will take global cooperation
From each and every nation
To ensure the asteroids won't destroy our Earth!

The Natural History Museum

Our LA Natural History Museum is a wonderful learning experience for all ages. I assisted for a while as a docent and was so pleased I learned so much about our natural history. We went on a variety of NHM excursions, and Charley and I both felt the experiences and leaders were exceptional.

Swirling Ammonites

In a growing circle the ammonite swirls around
Follow it back to its center and suddenly we are found
At the beginning of the cycle eons before man
Before the Earth was done evolving according to plan

Do you think the ammonite knew what it was doing?
As round it went, it seemed content not knowing what was brewing
That it would be caught in the swell of volcanoes and surges
So that it too became extinct as species went through purges

And so we see the precursor of other lowly creatures
Entombed and altered into stone with only certain features
Left from its early living state – the delicate spirals swirling
Seeming to move and undulate with its body curling

Ram's horns
on Egypt's Ammon god –
Strength spelling
future doom
Disaster waiting –
a lightning rod
As destruction loomed

Our minds can't begin to fathom its survival through the ages
Our fingers can slowly trace the shape but only imagine the stages
Of growth that it went through when it lived and what it condoned
Before it was a fossil – an ammonite turned to stone.

Puffed Up Rock

An asteroid that came to Earth
Caused us problems galore
It left a hole, for what it's worth,
And killed off the dinosaurs

Another one, or so we hear,
Just barely passed us by
48,000 miles is so near
It could hit us on the fly

It's good for us to check these rocks
'Cause them we want to avoid
We sure don't want to get a knock
From a rock that is on a *steroid*…!

Fool's Gold

"Fool's Gold" is what they call it
It shines so bright and clear
It really isn't gold, you see
But something else, my dear

Some say it can do good things
Like help our brains and breathing
And improve digestion
Of everything we're eating

It helps decrease negativity
Keeps us positive and wiser
By providing us warmth and protection
This "gold" won't make us misers

Real gold makes people greedy
It makes them lust for more
And turns them into monsters
Who'd do anything to score

Perhaps it isn't foolish
To want to have "fool's gold"
For our lives could be much better
When all is done and told.

Family

Poems about each of our families have been difficult to write. Charley's include three prior marriages – the first two ending in divorce, the third when she passed away. His first marriage was a "set-up." The mother of his first wife wanted her married after she had an abortion. She found brilliant Charley – an innocent recent graduate from MIT. He worked for the USAF as a rocket engineer, and she completed her degree in accounting. They had two children, and she became an alcoholic. She found someone else, divorced him, took the child support funds he provided, spent them on booze, and lied to the kids. She also prevented them from visits either way. He moved to California to continue working in the aerospace industry and met a psychologist to whom he was married for three years. She divorced him, and he was again blocked from connecting with their daughter. In later years she tried to split up their daughter's marriage. She then decided, since their daughter wouldn't listen, to murder the daughter and the two granddaughters, and then committed suicide. Needing a companion, Charlie married an older woman who had teenage daughters who gave him encouragement but also were manipulative. Charley and I found each other through the "Connections" dating service and were together 25 years.

Son David

Happy Birthday David

Today he would have been forty-six
With a keen sense of humor and prone to play tricks
On family and friends – like the April Fish …
It's good he got his greatest wish
To work with marine life
And lessen his strife
While increasing his knowledge
Going back to college

When I look at the tank that he built
Careful placement of filters to screen out the silt
I think that the fish swimming blithely around
Are thankful, as I am, that his knowledge was sound

Oh fish, how I wish he were still here with us
I'd laugh more at his jokes
Not make such a fuss…

Bonus Mom

In the late 1990s son David and Kelly Mulligan met at Westchester High School.

Musicians both –
David a drummer
Kelly a guitarist

Kelly was into the drug scene –
David was **not**
He told his colleagues that drugs
Inhibit your ability to play
And create music
And he and Kelly often argued

Before his motorcycle accident
Kelly told me that they had
Another argument about drugs

Kelly helped me find him
She was there for me
At his memorial service

Kelly wanted to change her life
Quit the drugs, attend programs
And get certified

Her mother was fed up
And wouldn't help her
So I drove Kelly to the meetings

During that time
Which lasted months
I helped her with job applications
And reference letters
She began to refer to me as
Her "Bonus Mom"

Years later Kelly still does
And she checks in on me
Weekly with a phone call
From her home in Mesquite, Nevada
Where I can hear the barks of the dogs
In the background where
She cares for them in her pet care business.

Niece Christina

Hang In There!

*Dedicated to my creative and artistic niece, Christina Gustafson,
and the glass wind chime she created*

As I look at the lovely wind chime hanging from the tree
I can't help but think of what it says to me
To consider the beauty that surrounds us all
The blue of the skies and the colorful ball
Of the hot air balloon which stands out loud and clear
It lets us all know that we should have no fear
Or even be shy about reaching for the sky
To attain our goals and keep aiming high
Your beautiful glass created with loving care
Is a reminder that we all need to **hang in there!**

The wind chime is hanging from a magnolia tree in the patio of my bungalow at Palm Court, a senior residence in Culver City. A photo is on my website: www.wordpainting.net. It seems to cheer up everyone who walks by – residents, staff, and visitors. Your thoughtfulness has brought joy to many people, including your Aunt Jan.

Pamela

I Had a Dream

I had a dream not long ago
It still stays in my head
In it I had a lovely child
Who clung to me with dread
She feared the fact that she was born
With her mother unmarried
It didn't matter to her
That for nine months she was carried
And that her birth mother spoke with her
And prayed she would be healthy
And that her life would be fulfilled
Perhaps she would be wealthy

First twenty years went flashing by
When her adoptive parents found me
We forged a link, but very weak
She didn't seem to know
How she could have two sets of parents
Who both could love her so

We saw each other from time to time
She married twice and then
Her second husband sent a picture
Of my grandson, Colin
When I called up and asked if I could send him Christmas presents
I was told that he already has two sets of grandparents
I wasn't needed in their lives… they shut me out completely

I have not seen my daughter now for close to seven years
She took herself out of my life but let me know about her son
She doesn't know for twenty years I used to shake with fear
When I would hear the story of a child molested, I'd pray that she wasn't the one.

Unwed Motherhood

A social pariah is what I was, so family members say
I had come home from France with a baby on the way
Mother was simply horrified that I could cause her such shame
All I heard from every side was that I carried blame

Blame for being pregnant, blame for letting it show
Blame for just existing, they were wishing I would go
Away as far as possible from every one of them
According to my family, I had committed the very worst sin

This was in the early '60s, puritanical even then
When everyone hid secrets, acted holier than sin

We, the unwed mothers, gave up children – every one
If we wanted to keep them, it simply wasn't done
Here in U.S. society, where one's social status mattered
Conceiving a child out of wedlock, I was lowest on the ladder

Because I wasn't married, my child had no father
And thinking at the time was not to even bother
With an unwed woman, to hide her was okay
Until she had the baby, and it was given away

I thought to seek an abortion but discovered it was too late
I found I had no choice, so resigned myself to my fate
To carry out the pregnancy, then return to normal life
Not knowing how this decision would cause me endless strife

I thought my family loved me, but now they cast me out
It did no good to talk to them; their deaf ears heard no shout

So I left them for the Northwest where I had finished college
And the family was convinced I didn't get much knowledge
I went to see the doctor I'd had when I was at school
He arranged for an adoption, those days it was the rule

I lived not far from campus, but avoided going there
Not wanting to meet old friends who really wouldn't care
Except to spread around the news: "Guess who I saw today!
Janet's come back into town, and she's in a family way!"

I worked as a temporary secretary; from job to job I'd go
Each time my girth would start to change, and I began to show
That I was really pregnant, and not just overweight

I'd ask the agency to find me another place
The last few months before the birth it was hard to get around
I finally had to quit my job and it was then I found
That I had no one to talk to except the child within
And I told her all my thoughts about her conception in sin

And I told her all my feelings about the love I lacked
From my parents and Dutch fiancée that led me to seek love in sex
I told her how I was to marry my Dutchman in the fall
Until he wrote and told me that he didn't love me at all

But that he preferred gentlemen, of his very own gender
So feeling I needed to prove myself, I went out on a bender
And had sex with a professor from the U.S. and Spain
I threw all caution to the winds; I didn't think I'd gain

A baby to take home with me, my souvenir from France
I guess I should have realized I didn't have a chance
To dodge the silver bullet that was aimed right at me
And that I'd have to deal with it and would never again be free

To live out all the dreams I'd had of loving and living in Holland
Instead I had to follow through, give birth and learn to swallow
The knowledge I was tainted, no longer a worthy daughter
A daughter now out on her own, a mother's child without her

Throughout the years I thought of her, I prayed she was OK
I'd hope that she wasn't one of those I read about each day
Who had been molested or harmed by sick adults
I hoped her adoptive parents had none of those faults

And then one night I had a call from her adoptive dad
He asked me if I'd like to meet the sweet young girl I'd had
He had been trying to find me since she had turned sixteen
She was having problems though she was a campus queen

He thought she needed closure about her ancestry
So I was invited to Washington to discuss the family tree
And for the very first time my daughter and I would meet
I could only hope it would be a happy occasion for me.

Meeting with Daughter

I went full of trepidation, not sure what to expect
She was turning twenty, about to graduate

Our meeting was very hurtful for I think she'd begun to hate
What she thought I had done to her; deserted her, you see
Never a thought that what I'd gone through had had any effect on me

For years we saw each other every once in a while
And when she decided to stop by, I rarely received a smile
I went to her second wedding, but then she stopped corresponding
It was not until I received a photo of her child from her husband that I knew
I had a grandchild – at that time a year old.

When I called her husband about keeping in touch with my grandson, he
said that Colin had enough grandparents, and I wasn't needed or wanted
Colin recently graduated from high school and is heading for college
He will be able to use the funds I gave him to increase his knowledge.

I know I grew in wisdom as my child grew in me
I learned just what it's like to be alone, you see.

Unwed Grandmotherhood

She never really understood how close we had become
After all, for nine long months we were really one
She was the only being who could share my day
I talked with her for hours and thought I heard her say
"I love you, Mom. Oh, yes, I do, for taking care of me
And I would like to grow up sitting on your knee"

I wish I could have kept her, but it was not to be
So she was adopted by another family
For at that time, a mother could not be unwed
Since her dad was married, it was my "fault" instead
So often I have wished that I had had a voice
But as my family told me, I really had no choice

We met again in later years when she graduated
From college with honors, which was anticipated
By her adoptive parents, both teachers just like me
Who gave support and lots of love so she could be free
To grow up and to fulfill any of her dreams –
That didn't happen the way she wanted…or so it seems

She divorced her husband, who was a drunk and beat her
Then she finally married her old high school sweetheart
They attended the funeral of my only other child
Her reaction was noncommittal and seemed to me quite mild
I was truly hoping that we could continue to meet
To keep our relationship going, for I was in desperate need

Of having a child close to me, now that my son was dead
But she stopped communication; I don't know what went on in her head
Then they sent me a card with a picture of their son
My only grandson, Colin, who at the time was one
When I asked if I could write him, I really learned the score
They said he had two sets of grandparents and didn't need one more

So I'm left without a daughter or a son to call my own
But I know I must forgive, although it is hard to condone
The way that I was treated by family and by "friends"
I doubt if there is much they can do to make amends
Yet today I love and nurture all the children that I can
And I smile and hug them as they call me "Grammy Jan."

*In 2021 when the Bishop for the SoCal ELCA was confirmed, I wrote her a poem.
It expresses my relief at knowing my child was living a full and happy life.*

Thanks for Being Lutheran

Back in the 1960s when I gave up my child
I thought God had abandoned me
And my reaction wasn't mild
I felt imprisoned – no longer free
I thought I should stop living
And put an end to my grieving
After my daughter was given to others
And I was no longer considered her mother
Although I could use my skills
I simply seemed to have lost my will
But I took up my teaching again
Not letting myself go astray with a whim
Staying on target to teach
But continually trying to reach
My feelings that had become so buried
Inside me – lost without God
Over the years, I prayed, and I hoped
That my daughter was being cared for and loved
Each time I heard of a child being mistreated
I feared for her safety and sent God an entreaty
To protect her and guide her throughout her life
And allow her to live without too much strife

Her wonderful adoptive parents found me when she was in her teens
I sent God a prayer of thanks and breathed a sigh of relief.

Pamela's Poems

Pamela was 16 when her adoptive parents, the Altmans, located me. I had been writing poetry for years and was delighted to find that Pamela was also a poet – and an excellent one. Here are some that she shared with me.

1

In the eventide of Spring
The moonbeams while away the hours,
Playing upon both leaf and twig.
Playing upon both leaf and twig.
Greets rusty brown and starlight fallen twinkles.
Behold, among the whispering trees and conspiring grasses
Float rainbow rings of damsels fair
Adorned with dewdrop sashes.
Adorned with dewdrop sashes.
In secret melodies the moonbeams chuckle.
Over grassy plains and forest greens their laughter does follow.

2

I dream, not that my dreams
may come true,
But that I may find truth
in my dreams.

3

Hate is malignant.
Feeding on diseased love,
it grows and multiplies.
Left unchecked,
it has the power to kill.

4

To Jenny
Why do I ponder the lost stories
of what might have been
Even if it is the right choice I have made
the possibilities of unchosen courses
seem endless
And in their endlessness – they are freedom
in the face of my own
Known consequences of choice.

5

Over the clouds I've traveled
fast against the sky
Skidding down uncut paths –
an accident of fate am I.
Scarred and broken; ailing in my youth
I have found myself diminished,
wings dangling at my feet.
In the shrouded silence,
I hear your call of faith.
My heart leaps as the pain becomes
bittersweet.

6

If I lived a thousand years
would oceans succumb to thirst
And sightless eyes see opaque skies
which once rained life on earth
No more the flight of ruffled feathered wings
nor shrieks of careless mirth
The meadows have forgotten green
The air takes not the breath of birth
O world that I once knew
a thousand years ago
You have deserted me
in this barren womb
of ice and snow

Charley's Family

Little Girls Lost

Dust to dust and ashes to ashes
We're all aware of how quickly life passes
But when young lives are cut short in their prime
Killed by fear and by hatred, it's a horrible crime
We still have our memories, the good and the bad
Remembering any will render us sad
Sad to dwell on what happened at such a great cost
Daughter and granddaughters; oh, what we've lost...!
So we focus on memories and cry as we must
Over children's remains now just ashes and dust.

Charley's second wife, a psychologist, was angry with their daughter because she refused to listen to her when she tried to make her break up with her husband. She took matters into her own hands and killed the daughter (38) and the two granddaughters (two and four), then committed suicide. On 12/18/2009 the grandchildren were buried, and the daughter's ashes were scattered at sea on 1/2/2010. Let us always remember the unpredictability of life and cherish our loved ones while we can.

Are You Sleeping God?

Where are you, God? Have you been sleeping?
Aren't you aware of all our weeping?
The count of dead children has risen to four
Now, I wonder, will there be more?

It's hard to believe it was 10 years ago
When we received the very first blow
With news of son David's accidental death
Which left us both shaken and bereft

Now a daughter and two granddaughters are dead
Come on, God, where is Your head?
Why not take us, we're infirm and old
Is it too much to ask? Are we being too bold?

Two lovely granddaughters are with us still
Now a great grandson, who makes our hearts fill
With love and prayers, for he is in Your keeping
So please, Lord, protect them, and keep us from weeping.

Grammy to Lots of Kids

Charley's son, Howard, had a daughter, Sarah Ellen Hoult, who married Richard Murphy. For many years we did what we could to provide assistance for them by giving them cars, additional funds, etc. Sarah was angry when I sent her a note expressing concern that Howard would attempt to bad-mouth Charley at the memorial service, so we made him part of the flag ceremony with the mayor and a Culver City friend. Sarah was not happy and cut her connection with me.

When Howard married again, he inherited three boys. He provided assistance for his wife, Sue, and the boys. He taught the eldest, Matthew, how to drive a tow truck. The other two focused on what they wanted to achieve. Jeremy became a firefighter and James an educator, a counselor giving assistance to high school students who need guidance as they make their decision to continue their studies. They are our step-grandkids, and we have many more who looked at both of us as grandparents. I'm still referred to as Grammy by former students and by those who have become step-grandkids.

Advice to the Grandchildren

from Grammy Jan

Others may try to keep you still
Or make you act against your will

Holding you back in cage or mind
As you continue your struggle to find

Your way in a world with so many choices
While being bombarded by dozens of voices

Coming at you from every direction
Trying to push you to make a selection

That you may not want to do with your life
That you may find just adds to your strife

So stick with your prayers, stay true to your course
For in years to come, things could get worse

Just keep your mind clear and your head in the fight
It's better to do what you think is right

But if you decide to take advice from another
Make sure you listen to your loving grandmother.

Janet's Early Travels

Before sharing more about my travels with Charley, I thought I'd mention my affinity for things that take us places, such as cars, planes, ships, and even my own two feet that took me dancing at a prestigious French ball. I remember those times very well, and the subject of "time" also brought to mind my so-called Rolex watch.

Travels
Before we begin our jaunts, I thought I'd let you know a bit about
my affinity for things that take us places – cars, trains, ships,
planes, hot air balloons, zip-lines!

Learning to Drive

When we came back to the U.S. from Iran
Dad decided I needed to learn how to drive since I was now 17
We had a 1949 Chevrolet with a gear shift
Manual drive
We lived in the Virgina countryside
In a house with a driveway bordered by a telephone pole
And garbage cans

I did quite well when driving on the straight road up and down the hill
Shifting gears and slowing down
But when it came time to turn into the driveway
I turned too soon to the left and hit the telephone pole
I backed up to try again, but turned too far to the right
And hit the garbage cans
The noise was such a shock, I backed into the ditch
Dad had to call a tow truck
And told me that was the end of my driving lessons
I didn't get my driver's license until I was a senior in college
Guess I needed a bit more knowledge…!

Flying High

When I was living in France
I thought I'd take a chance
To go sky high
And learn to fly

How I loved the feeling
And my senses weren't reeling
So I learned
And I earned
My wings!

Then I discovered gliders and sailplanes
Golden silence sat well on my brain
So I decided to make a shift
And learn to fly them, if you get my drift

Hot air balloons are what call me these days
Floating in silence when gas sounds fade
Going low and flying high
Still way up in the sky

What a joy to be sky high!

In the 1960s when I was on a Fulbright fellowship in France, I was invited to the 9th Ball honoring the Legion of Honor in Perigueux, Dordogne. It was quite a ceremony – I won a Sevres vase donated by the President of the Republique, Charles de Gaulle, and had a delightful time dancing the twist! Take a peek at the photo on my website, WordPainting.net.

Le Twist

Turning our bodies
From one side to the other
We show we can move
Them from head to toe
In doing so
We control them you know
Twisting and turning
With body parts burning
All parts are moving
Our bodies are grooving
They follow our notions
As we keep them in motion
To the music's time
With our bodies in rhyme
From side to side
We delight in the ride
With our heads, feet, and wrists
While dancing
"Le Twist!"

The Queen and I

The Queen and I are of an age
When dancing swing was all the rage
In '36 we both were launched
Our early years were sure not staunched
For we both traveled the wide world over
Although our lives weren't steeped in clover
She carried troops in World War II
I worked with refugees in Beirut
She sailed the oceans from beach to beach
I went where I could study and teach
In Europe, the Middle East, and Asia
I found study and teaching quite a pleasure

We were both old at 75
I was glad I was still alive
And the Queen showed absolutely no restraint
All decked out in her new coat of paint
Now we're both celebrating the age of 80
And hoping we both keep on feeling great
Her building began, or so I've been told,
In '34, making her two years old…er!
I laughed and said that had to be wrong
And someone needs to sing a new song
For I can certainly say without hesitation
The Queen launched after 24 months of gestation
In 1936 we both emerged with forms quite fine
Although the months to mold me just totaled nine!

ROLEX!?

Back in the 1980s I taught for USC in their master's degree program on U.S.
Army bases in Korea and Japan
When I was in Korea, a U.S. Army general asked me for a date
I agreed and the camaraderie was great
When it was time for me to return to the States
He gave me a lovely watch to remember him by
With hope that we would see each other again some time.
That ROLEX watch has become my very favorite
I do remember him each time I look at it
But we never saw each other again
When I took it to ANYTIME*
To get a new battery installed
I was told by the proprietors that the watch
With which I was enthralled
Was made in Korea and really a FAUX LEX…not a ROLEX!
I guess it underscored that my relationship with the general
Was not real but actually FAUX …
Oh well, what can I say?
I still enjoy wearing my "ROLEX" every day!

*ANYTIME, Culver City, CA

Culver City – An Inspiration

Ode To Janet

*By Sandra Coopersmith, June 9, 2018
on the launch of Janet's
"Culver City Centennial Collection"*

Janet has been referred to
As the Energizer Bunny.
Well, she does gets things done
And on that you can bet money.

When she became Poet Laureate
She didn't just sit back and bask.
Instead, she spearheaded
A multitude of tasks.

At city council meetings
Her poems would delight,
Adding a special flavor
To the menu of the night.

She organized poetry readings
To creatively celebrate
Our wonderful city's Centennial
On several memorable dates.

The popular poetry readings
She presented were really neat.
They nourished mind and body
Since people got to listen *and* eat!

Getting this book together and launched
Was a labor of love (no argument there);
It took tons of her time and effort
But Janet is someone who cares

So please join me in applauding
This fiercely dedicated soul –
Our fantastic Poet Laureate
Who met her ambitious goal –
Yay, Janet!

During the over 50 years I've lived in Culver City, as I grew older I became bolder and involved myself in many Culver City activities – boards, committees, organizations, events – to support our community. Being named "Older American" to represent Culver City in 2022 gave me the opportunity to remind us all about the importance of our elderly citizens!

2022 Memory Inspiration

Who knew
That in 2022
"Older American"
Would be added to my name
And became
Sort of a claim
To fame!

It meant I couldn't reverse my age any more
That everyone now knew the score
And made me realize now that I was older
I definitely had to be bolder!

So in 2023 I decided to get out of my rut
Got my hair and nails cut
Made sure I had my mask
In case anyone asked…

Juiced up my motor scooter
And headed for the Senior Center
To a concert during the day
Because at night there would be no way!

Maybe being referred to
As Culver City's Older American for 2022
And realizing that I was indeed older
Has made me much bolder
Encouraging others
To begin
Sharing
The title
With me
In 2023…!

Sharing with Charley

Charley asked to be brought home from the hospital knowing he would soon be gone. He visited with family and friends while he lay on a gurney in the living room looking at a large photo of a place we had visited called "The Eye of God" (now with Pastor Jim). Charley and I shared our likes and dislikes and beliefs. We supported each other in so many things, including politics. Charley went with me to the Culver City city council meetings. He read my poems and remarks beforehand, gave me suggestions, and cheered me on as he did with this one.

What's in a Name – Congress

Have you ever watched baboons cavorting at a zoo?
They can be quite obnoxious and idiotic too
They're viciously aggressive and not so very smart
I've heard people wonder if the species has a heart
But there is another group with an equal claim to fame
With some very similar traits and the same collective name
Baboons are not a monkey tribe. Would you care to take a guess?
They share their collective name with a human group – Congress

I've been told that salamanders are called a Congress too
Perhaps that's appropriate for all the things they do
They're known to be quite slippery and hard to hold on to
With mucus on their bodies that doesn't act like glue
They might even remind you of politicians you know
If you should catch their tails or legs, they'll gladly let them go
For they will grow another to replace it in a day
So although you may catch them, they slither right away…

Soon there will be another election
Let's be very careful about our selection
Baboons or salamanders should not be our choice
We need to speak with a concerted voice
Casting our votes for those who aim high
Like an eagle which takes us to the sky
For you see eagles are called a Congress too
And we need more to watch over me and you
So cast your vote and make it clear
When we elect eagles, we need have no fear
We will know the score
And with eagles we'll soar.

Travels With Charley

During our 25 years together, Charley and I traveled all over the world to see solar eclipses, with his student Rocket Engineers from CSULB and CSULA, as well as visiting many countries and places.

Big Bear

Charley and I had a vacation home in Big Bear that we enjoyed for many years. We were there in 1991 when the 6.5 earthquake hit. As residents of Culver City, we had become members of CERT – the Community Emergency Response Team – where we learned how to turn off the gas, which we did for the Big Bear homes that were vacant. Getting training from CERT can help keep our communities safer in all kinds of weather as we work together. Knowledge is power, especially when the power goes out!
In 1991 Big Bear became known as "Chimney Falls," and we wanted to make sure it didn't get a more fiery nickname. As the current inhabitants deal with the snow, perhaps there's another nickname in the works – "Frosty the Big Bear"??

Quaking in Big Bear??

Back in 1991
We had gone to Big Bear to have some fun
To celebrate our anniversary
When the first quake hit Landers, we felt an aftershock
And called family saying we were OK
When the second shock hit
The TV fell out of the wall and landed between us on the bed
Everything from the shelves in the kitchen was on the floor
The glass top table was split in half
And yet
We were OK
We checked the house, foundations, electricity, gas
Then realized that most of our neighbors were not there
We had completed our training with our Culver City
Community Emergency Response Team and had our tools with us
After we checked our house, we went around the neighborhood
Checked on other folks who were there
And went to the homes that were empty to turn off the gas
To make sure they didn't go up in flames
There wasn't much we could do with the chimneys that fell
For a while Big Bear was known as "Chimney Falls."

A Memorable Winter in Big Bear

Each winter we went up to our cabin in Big Bear
And took our dogs along, sometimes a pair
Our dogs were part of our family, you know
And enjoyed visiting our cabin and the snow

One year we had a brand-new puppy
A Boxer puppy Charley named Pepper
When joining our calm Yellow Lab, Sunshine
Pepper showed us *her* name was just fine!

It was going to be very cold up there
So we bought Pepper a sweater to wear
Pepper let us know it was not to her taste
She kept nipping at it around her waist

Pepper dragged behind almost needing a tow
When we took a very short walk in the snow
With the fire out in the fireplace we left her sweater on
In the morning we found that the sweater was "gone"

Sunshine let us know that something wasn't right
Pepper had been very naughty overnight
She had not yet learned to do what she was told
And Sunny couldn't keep Pepper under control

Pepper greeted us both with a big grin on her face
The sweater was off, no longer in place
She'd managed to wriggle out of it during the night
Pee-peed all over it, and her face showed her delight…!

Las Vegas

Goose Eggs

Winter is the time of year we think of Christmas goose
Instead, we see the goose-necked cranes coming home to roost
After wild abundance of the free-spending economy
We find that we have overspent and lost financial harmony

The goose-necked cranes are standing still, stark against the skies
Over buildings not complete whose windows' empty eyes
Look out on a different world than when the jobs began
And construction work was booming, following a plan

In other times, they did their dance and moved with awkward grace
And we would watch them lift and strain to put the beams in place
Now, silently, they stand alone with empty hanging cables
While idle workers hope that they can put food on their tables

For those of us who still have jobs and wherewithal to live
This Christmas let's remember those who do without and give
Our time and what we can afford to help them struggle through
With dreams and hopes that next year will bring better times anew.

Russia

A Prayer to St. Catherine, Patron Saint of Maidens

In the spring of 2007, while my husband and I were on a cruise down the inland waterways of Russia, I was reminded of this poem I had heard more than 50 years ago. I could only recall parts of it, but later research after we returned to the U.S. led me to the complete version.

St Catherine, St Catherine, oh lend me thine aid,
And grant that I never may die an old maid.
A husband, St Catherine, a *good* one, St Catherine;
Handsome, St Catherine, *rich*, St Catherine.
But anyone's better than no one, St Catherine.

We were stopping to visit many towns, churches, and monasteries en route from St. Petersburg to Moscow. At one of the monasteries, a guide showed us icons dedicated to St. Catherine, the patron saint of maidens and spinsters, and remarked that he didn't think any Americans were familiar with St. Catherine. I told him I had heard a poem to St. Catherine long ago that listed the attributes a maiden wanted in a husband.

Later that day, back on board the ship, passengers were preparing to put on a "show," and I decided to develop my own poem to St. Catherine to recite based upon what I could remember. As I put my Russian shawl over my head, I asked the audience to stretch their imaginations and think of me (at 71) as a young maiden while I said my prayer to St. Catherine.

*Adapted by Dr. Janet Hoult
from a poem vaguely remembered from 50 years ago!*

St Catherine, St Catherine, oh, please hear my prayer
Bring me a husband, but let him have hair…!
Make his eyes like an eagle, his nose like a beak
But, St Catherine, St Catherine, please let him have teeth…!

Make him tall, make him handsome, make him kind, make him rich
But without any lice, so he doesn't itch…!

Make him strong as an ox, a man among men
But let him be able to count higher than ten…!

Oh, St Catherine, St Catherine, do all that you can
But, St. Catherine, St. Catherine, please bring me a man…!

Russian Birches

Tall sentinels along the Volga
Long branches drooping and sighing
Leaves drifting moss-like in the wind

Standing tall
Yet feeling the weight of history
The great drama of Russia

Bark spotted with black
Not pure and white
But burned and scarred by life and events

Thick underbrush guarding deep secrets
The silver birches welcome, but they dare you to come
These sentinels on guard against the interloper.

Portugal

Cork Trees

The tree
beckons with
its two-toned trunk
the color of mahogany
where the bark has been cut away
the upper still holding close its thick gray bark.
We have come upon a grove of Portuguese cork trees
twisted, as though they want to protect their treasure,
but yielding, like the cork made from their bark,
with limbs reaching out as if they know
their cork will bring pleasure.
Perhaps they are saying
"Here,   take   what I
have   made   for you
and   enjoy."   As we
do   when we open
a bottle   of wine
sniff the cork
and fill
ourselves
with the
aroma
captured
by the
wondrous
cork.

Spain

Say What????

My husband and I like to travel
But sometimes things start to unravel
Since we both don't hear well
And we find we must spell
A word that is different or novel

For example, what happened in Spain
When I found that I had to explain
That the restaurant served tapas
And the servers weren't topless
Bet he won't make that mistake again!

Solar Eclipses

Where Did the Sun Go?

Eclipses have happened for eons, long before scientific truths
Around the world and over the years, explanations were legends and myths
Early Greeks thought they were abandoned by the Sun in the darkened sky
Their word for "abandon" is "eclipse," which we've used without knowing why
There are many myths and legends from places the whole world over
So hold on to your hats and get ready to fly; we have the globe to cover!

When the moon's orbit
takes it between the Earth and the Sun,
the shadow that falls on the Earth
makes it seem that the Sun has partially or totally disappeared.

Creatures on the Earth react the increasing darkness
in many ways - cows return to the barn thinking it is nightfall
and the night insects begin their singing.

At First Contact,
it looks like a small bite has been taken out of the Sun.
The temperature begins to drop;
crescent shadows and shadow bands appear on the ground.
Before an Eclipse reached Totality,
light from the Sun peeks through the
Valleys on the edge of the Moon ... Baily's Beads.
As the shadow gradually moves,
the last of the Beads appears like a Diamond Ring.
Then, in a Total Solar Eclipse,
the Sun's Corona surrounds a great dark eye
We have night during the day until, after a few minutes,
the shadow begins to move and we have Final Contact.

Islands

There it is! Can you see it?
A spot on the horizon
Floating on the ocean
Seeming to drift in a haze

What do islands remember
Of those who called them home
The survivors of the Bounty
Who from Pitcairn did not roam

And those on Easter Island
Who left moai statues for us to find
To see these stone creations
Can really blow your mind!

Then we think of islands
Like the Hawaiian five
Each with special features
That keep our spirits alive

Waterfalls, pineapple, and beaches
Just to name a few
Are you ready to go on a trip
To an island? Let's do it! Just find us a ship!

*Islands hold memories that help us.
One of our eclipse trips took us through the South Pacific where we visited Easter Island and the stone statues ("moai") as well as meeting a descendant of Fletcher Christian (Tom – great, great, great, great grandson), who came on board to greet us from Pitcairn Island.*

Hawaiian Melodies I'll Remember

Hawaiian melodies
Can infuse your mind with joy
Even though the song is sad
The music makes you feel glad

Glad to be alive
Wanting to continue to thrive
And keep on striving
To add hope to other's lives

For many years I enjoyed my ukulele
Playing and rehearsing at home
With Charley listening and letting me know
Which were his favorite songs

He especially liked Don Ho's Hawaiian songs
Which our Culver City Strummers
Included often in their performances –
Where no song was ever wrong

As part of Charley's memorial service
Accompanied by Cali Rose
I serenaded him by singing Don Ho's
"I'll Remember You."

Kobe - Limerick

One of our solar eclipse trips was a cruise that took us to Japan. I'd written other poems about the eclipses and decided to focus on the places we visited. Kobe was one of them.

In Kobe you find lots of ships
And beef which slides over your lips
But so much congestion
Can cause indigestion
And add even more to your hips!

Losing Charley

The Field of Reeds

During the years I lived in the Middle East, I had the opportunity to visit Egypt on many occasions, including the pyramids – not only Cheops, but also Saqqara – and to learn about the religious beliefs in ancient times. When Charley and I were on a total solar eclipse trip, we went to Cairo before going to Libya. Unfortunately, he had a heart attack and wound up in a Cairo hospital. By the time he was released, it was too late to join the eclipse group. Since Charley had never visited Egypt we hired a car, took our AstroScan telescope, and visited at least two pyramids – Cheops and Saqqara – the step pyramid and one of the oldest with an incredible history.
We got to Saqqara and set up the scope. Charley was in his element, showing folks the 85% view of the eclipse and explaining it to them. They didn't need special mylar glasses but could view it through the AstroScan.

Many came to view the partial eclipse
and some shared with us
religious beliefs about death
that had been taught in ancient Egypt.
In Saqqara they learned about
what happened when you
passed to the other side.
Ancient Egyptians believed that
the first place you went to acclimate yourself
was the Field of Reeds.
It was there you began to determine
which path you would take
in the afterlife.

After Charley died, I went to see a medium.
She told me that Charley was holding
what looked like a piece of grass
and that he was waving it.
I recognized it as a reed, and that he was letting me know he was there
in the Field of Reeds, where he would be until he moved on.
The next time I saw the medium
she told me he was trying on different shoes.
He had always said that he would like to
get to know others
and walk in their shoes…

Touching

As your fingertips touch the edge of my hand, I feel a sense of joy
It's not the same as once it was when we were girl and boy
Your touch now makes me feel secure and cherished in a way
I know that you will care for me and I for you each day

Though our skin's no longer smooth, and our hands are rough
Gentle touches that we give are never quite enough
As your strong and competent hand gently caresses mine
I know that no matter what happens everything will be fine

We both know that as we go through the years together
Many storms will come our way that we'll successfully weather
No matter what the future holds we will not need too much
For we can both feel secure in each other's touch.

On Tuesday, we brought Charley home from the hospital, and he passed away in our living room from Acute Myeloid Leukemia the following morning, the day before Thanksgiving. I walked into the room just before 5:00 AM.

I touched his hand, then put my hand upon his heart – it was still beating
I kissed his cheek, and I could tell he was still breathing
I lifted my hand and stepped back from the bed
His breathing stopped – and he was dead…
He had waited for me to say "Goodbye"
That it was OK for him to die
Now though I'm sad and filled with sorrow
He's made it easier to face tomorrow
For I know his love is with me still and that his pain has ceased
We've helped each other through the years and found our ways to peace.

After the memorial service at Grace Lutheran Church in Culver City most of his ashes were scattered at sea, but at the Intercollegiate Rocket Engineering Competition the following June, some were placed in the Cal State Long Beach rocket his Experimental Sounding Rocket Association students built, and Charley's ashes were scattered in the atmosphere when the parachute was deployed after the launch.

Countdown: 5-4-3-2-1 – Lift Off …!

Charley Sets Sail

Inspired by Henry Van Dyke's
"Gone From My Sight"

My dear Charley took many trips
By car, on planes, and sometimes ships
I like to think that Van Dyke's lines
Were written just with him in mind

He compared death to a ship sailing
With folks like Charley at the railing
While we on shore wave 'til she's gone
Our hearts emptied of their songs

Yet as his ship grows small in size
It's only in our hearts and eyes
For as it reaches the distant shore
He'll be met by those who've gone before

So we wish you "Godspeed" from this end
Your loving family, your colleagues and friends
Knowing in our hearts you'll have a smooth ride
And a warm welcome waiting for you on the other side.

Folks have asked if they can use the poem, and I give them my blessing.
It seems to provide hope for many, and when we lose a loved one, a smile is always welcome.

Unexpected Note

While sorting through papers
I found a note
That Charley wrote
Not long after we were married
And the sentiment it carried
Has stayed with me all these years

How glad I was that I quieted my fears
And agreed that we should marry
We had 25 years together
And what he wrote
In his unexpected note
Will be with me forever.

Dearest Jan,

Well, I'm here at work, and I won't get much done until I write this little billet-doux – I can't get you off my mind.

The thing is, while it's always there, the intensity of my feeling for you varies from time to time. This morning at breakfast, it was quiet. Now (9:45), consuming, a roar. The unity of us/we envelops me. And that cherishing thing you have felt – that I feel for you very strongly right now. I love us!

It's glorious stuff.

Charley

Acknowledgments

- Christina Gustafson - my niece - who helped me revise and finalize this manuscript. Without her assistance, I could not have completed "Journeys with Charley and Beyond."
- Isabella Stehlin - Organizer, fine-tuner and UCLA student
- Sandra Coopersmith – Editor
- Grammy's "kids" – especially my step-grandkids who are my trustees: James Smith, counselor at Culver City High School, and his brother, Jeremy Smith, firefighter and EMT with LAFD
- The Culver Arts Foundation for all they do to support the arts in Culver City
- Culver City Crossroads and Judith Martin-Straw for providing continued support of Culver City and a venue for valuable information
- The Green Poets of Beyond Baroque for providing suggestions to make my poems stronger
- The Painting with Words Zoom group made of up of many of my former students in the Word Painting with Poetry class at the Culver City Senior Center for their encouragement
- The staff and residents at Palm Court, my new senior residence, for their support as I completed the manuscript
- Grace Lutheran Church for continued support, encouragement, and prayers through the years
- Culver City, which has been my home and homebase for over 50 years as I made my academic travels.
  - Thank you for recognizing the Art that is in the heArt of our city.
  - Thank you for all you have done and continue to do to support all our citizens, including the disabled and the elderly.

As I begin my 87th year, it is an honor to call Culver City my home.

Janet Cameron Hoult
Author

Professor Emerita at California State University, Los Angeles and Culver City's Poet Laureate Emerita, Janet has lived and traveled all over the world: high school in Iran, universities in Lebanon, France, and the United States, and teaching assignments in Germany, Korea, Japan, Thailand, China, and Costa Rica. Now in her 80s, Dr. Hoult is reviewing her life and writing her autobiography – her memoir – with poetry and anecdotes. Ashes of her husband, Charley, a rocket scientist, were dispersed by his Cal State Long Beach students at the 2017 IREC at Spaceport America in New Mexico. The first two books, "Jaunts with Janet" and "Juggling with Janet," take you through her first 60 years. "Journeys with Charley and Beyond" continues the story of their life together and how Janet has kept on keeping on as she nears her 90s.

Isabella Stehlin
Organizer – Fine Tuner

Isabella Stehlin of Culver City, California is currently a second-year student at UCLA, where she is pursuing a degree in Ecology, Behavior, and Evolution. Her goal is to work in the field of conservation. In her spare time, she fosters orphaned kittens and enjoys hiking along the coastal shores and mountainous terrain of her home state.

Sandra Coopersmith
Editor

A Culver City resident since 1983, a friend, a poet, a journalist, and an excellent editor, she has been features writer for Culver City News, Culver City Crossroads, and Culver City Observer, and in 2015 received certificates of recognition from the City of Los Angeles and the California State Assembly for the public service provided by her two-part story in 2014 about fraud prevention. Freelance editing, cartooning, and volunteering are also on her slate of activities.

Printed in the USA
CPSIA information can be obtained
at www.ICGtesting.com
LVHW060258270424
778612LV00004B/30